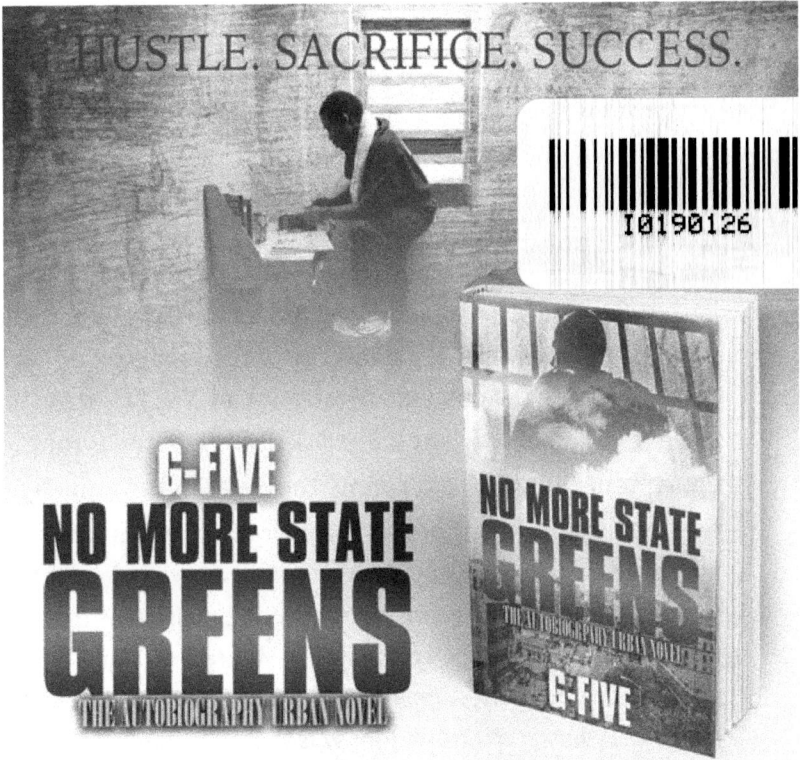

No More State Greens

HUSTLE. SACRIFICE. SUCCESS.

I0190126

G-FIVE
NO MORE STATE
GREENS
THE AUTOBIOGRAPHY URBAN NOVEL

NO MORE STATE
GREENS
THE AUTOBIOGRAPHY URBAN NOVEL
G-FIVE

#NOMORESTATEGREENS

PROLOGUE

MAY 2, 2012 3:30PM

1.   Baby wake up! The Police at the door! Those was the words
coming out of my wife mouth that snap me right out of my dream
into my worst nightmare of reality. As I got up & went to the door,
sure enough in my hallway stood 7 New York undercover
detectives from the narcotics division squad. The first thing that
came to my mind was that these dick heads is at the wrong
apartment, but little did I know they weren't. As much as I
hate to admit it, the Tactic's the police department use's to
apprehend a suspect without a warrant is very cunning. Before I
jumped into this drug game, I was taught 2 main rules that I lived
by which is #1 (Never sell crack where you rest at) and #2 (never
get high on your own supply), so not at one time did I think that the
narc's that was at my front door was there for me. They started out
asking me a few questions, like what was my name & who else was
in the house besides my wife & me. I told them my government
name & let them know that nobody else was there but just us, and
my 2 year old son. After telling them my name I was asked to show
some identification. I told my wife to grab my I.D out of my wallet
and bring it to me. I was then asked to step out into the hallway at
the time I didn't see anything wrong so I did. After being properly
identified I was place under arrest for 10 counts of criminal sells of
a controlled substance `220.41`.

CHAPTER 1

AUGUST 28, 1995 8:49PM

As the A Train pulls inside the station I eagerly waited for the doors to open up on 42nd street. As soon as both doors ajar I rushed off the cart in full speed bumping into passengers getting on & off the train. At the time I really didn't care, I had a bus to catch and getting to the Port Authority was the only thing on my mind. I still had about 11 minutes left before my bus departed at 9:00pm. At the age of 19 I was living life on the edge. I was already running the streets heavy, partying, playing with guns & selling drugs. I also had a big responsibility to take on and that was being a father to an 8 pound 6 ounces baby boy who was at the time 7 months old. That was the turning point in my life I had to step it up in the game & New York City wasn't cutting it so I took my hustle to another state. I started out traveling back & forth out of town transporting drugs. I had big plans for the State of Connecticut & getting rich was one of them. With no luggage, just the cloths I had on my back & a pocket full of drugs I was on my way. As I race through the Port Authority running behind schedule I still needed to purchase my bus ticket, but with 7 minutes left and 3 customers on line ahead of me there was no way in hell I was making that 9:00pm bus to New Britain C.T. As I approached the ticket counter the clock on the wall read 9:03pm. Behind the ticket counter stood a short Hispanic female about 5"4 with long jet black hair. I admit she was gorgeous, but her attitude was fucked up and nasty. By the looks of it she was having a bad day, but I didn't care so was I. I politely asked her was it any way possible for her to find out if the 9:00pm Greyhound to New Britain C.T departed yet, if not was it even possible for her to have them hold for at least 5 more minute's. Without even taking her eyes off the computer screen her direct words to me was no she can't, that's not part of her job description. Normally I would have had something smart to say but with a pocket full of drugs i didn't want to draw any unnecessary attention to myself so I politely said thank you & for her to have a nice day. As I turn to walk away from the ticket counter the mood of her attitude must have change in a split of a second, because just 1 minute ago this same lady was acting like she didn't want to be bothered now was willing to help me out. She let me know that it was a 9:30pm Bonanza going to Boston that stops in Hartford Connecticut arrival time 12:30am will I be willing to catch that bus. Being that New Britain is only 20 minutes away from Hartford I jumped right on it. The only difference was the price on the ticket, which was only $10.00 extra. After I paid for my ticket she let me know what gate my bus was departing from and I had about 15 minutes before it departed. Since I had 15 minutes to spare I made a quick stop at a concession stand located inside the Port Authority. I wasn't really hungry, so I just grab a Tropicana orange juice, 2 bags of Doritos potatoes chips and one of those Source Hip Hop magazines. When you are transporting drugs their is no special way to go about it either you going to get caught or you not, simple as that. Most people use mules to carry their drugs, females especially. For some reason people think females is the least, too be suspected, which is true some of the time but not all the time. Females tend to get nervous under pressure especially if it, have anything with them going to jail. The first thing police say to them is that they going to take away their kids if they don't cooperate. That's their breaking point. Now you do have a few that will hold it down those are what we call that ride or die chick. It can be your girlfriend, that side chick, or even that neighborhood hood rat that's just down for whatever for a couple of dollars. Me personally I would never put a love one especially my girlfriend in that type of situation to transport any type of drugs for me, now that hood rat that's a

4

different story. The only problem with them hood rat chicks is that they're never around when you really need them. Like this one chick from the hood name Keisha (aka) key-key she's down for whatever as long as you talking dollar signs. She's that one chick every drug dealer in the hood goes to when they need a crib to cook or bag up their drugs in. See Key-Key was a perfect example of a crack baby born in the 80's. Both of her parents was crack heads, her mother died giving birth to her little brother when she was 2 years old which left her to be raise by her grandmother. Her so called father never looked at her twice. By the time Key-Key turn 13 years old she was so out of control her grandmother had giving up on her. She was too much to handle, rumor was that Key-Key started turning tricks & fucking niggas for cash. Ever since she was young, Key-Key always found a way to make some money. But today like I said she's know where to be found. They always say if you want something done the right way you have to do it yourself. So here am walking through the Port Authority with a pocket full of drugs and before I even get to the gate I'm approached by 3 Port Authority Police getting off the escalator. I'm not going to even front I was nervous ass hell and that weed I smoked 2 hours prior didn't make it no better. That African Black I copped from 124th & Madison had my eyes blood shot red. At the time I was 19 years old but I had a face of a 16 years old kid. I had no facial hair on my face at all. They must have thought I was some type of runaway wondering around the Port Authority because the first question they ask me was where was my parents. I gave them the type of look like (what the fuck is you talking about) I'm 19 years old my mother is home. They must have thought I was lying about my age because as soon as I told them my age they ask me for some identification. At the time all I had on me was my old ass High School I.D, which had my date of birth on it, which had expired 2 years ago. After showing them I was old enough, they wanted to know where was I headed which I stated to them back home to Connecticut. They wanted to know what was I doing in NYC if I lived in C.T? I answered every fucking question they ask but they could tell I was a little bit nervous which I was. The only thing on my mind was to take off running but I thought maybe I could talk my way out of it. They must have sense I was about to take off on them so they surrounded me just in case I made any moves. I definitely wasn't about to catch an assault on police so I just stood my grounds and didn't run. I didn't know it at the time but the police needed probable cause to even search me, which they didn't have. They took it upon themselves to start going through my pockets where they found me carrying a large amount of crack cocaine. I was placed under arrest and charged with possession of a control substance with the intent to sell 220.16.

CHAPTER 2

I was taken to the Precinct which was located right there inside of the Port Authority where I was booked, fingerprinted and had my picture taken. I sat there for about 5 hours before being transported down to Central Booking. Central Bookings is located further down in mid-town Manhattan on 100 Centre Street. That's the place where they take you before you get arraign by a Judge for your case. It's like another screening process they put you through to see if you have any other warrants in any other state besides NYC. After arriving to central bookings I just knew I was in for a long 72 hour stay, that place was packed to the capacity, it looked like they had half of NYC locked up that night and it was only a Monday better yet early Tuesday morning. It was bodies everywhere, you had people sleeping on the floors, under benches, on top of the benches it was crazy, it wasn't even no room to stand up in there and this was going on in every cell. This wasn't my first time going through the system so I knew the whole procedure. There's a person that comes around asking you a bunch of questions pertaining to your background history. That determine if the Judge going to give you a bail or release you on your own recognizance. In my case I just knew I was getting a bail, not because of my background history but because of the charges. This was a class B felony I was facing and I was already out on R.O.R from an open case in Orange County. Around 6am that morning I had my interview and 2 hours after that they started clearing out cells moving people upstairs for morning courts. I got to central bookings around 3am that morning so I knew I wasn't seeing the judge no time soon I'll be lucky if I catch night court. I sat in that same cell for about 6 more hours surrounded by junkies. I swear to you dope fiends, is the worst people to be around when you locked up. They get this morning sickness that have their body going through all types of shit. Besides throwing up all over the place, they make this moaning sound constantly through the day and night while they sleeping. New York City is a great place to visit but really you don't want to live here. It seems like all, the NYPD do is lock people up all day long. As fast as they clear a cell out before the day is through it's right back filled up again. People be arguing over the phones, fighting for seats you name it they going through it. The night came and went. I didn't make night court but I was moved finally upstairs closer to seeing the Judge. The cells upstairs was a little cleaner but they was also smaller then the pens downstairs. That following morning I was finally assigned an Attorney she was an older white female her name was Elaine Matters. After discussing my case over with her she inform me that the officers is saying that they thought I was a runaway that's the reason for them stopping me but they didn't have probable cause to search me. She also was going to try and get me a bail as low as possible, if R.O.R wasn't an option since I had no real criminal history. At 1pm the courts shut down for an hour and a half for lunch. I was starving, I haven't ate nothing, for about 2 days but I'll be dam if I eat them hard ass cheese sandwiches they give us. The bread, be old & so cold plus the cheese is harder then a brick. If you never been locked up in NYC before then it's two things you should know, never eat them court sandwiches and never take a shit in them toilets that's in them cells. So to avoid all that don't eat them sandwiches. Courts resumed at 2:30pm and around 4:30pm my case was finally called. I was arraigned on possession of a controlled substance with the intent to sell, where the District Attorney asked for a $5000.00 dollar bail. I was then ask to put in a plea of guilty or not guilty for the charges that was being brought up against me which I stated not guilty. My lawyer then argued the fact that this was my first felony and I have no criminal history at the time. She then argue for me to be release on my own recognizance since the police didn't have probable cause and that it was an illegal search. The District Attorney mention I was already out on an open case which was a criminal possession of a weapon in the 3rd degree and for me to be held on bail which the judge granted for only $1500.00 dollars. I was then escorted back to the cells where I waited to be transported over to (MDC) Manhattan Detention Complex better known as the Tombs. Each borough has there own correctional facility except for Staten Island. The Bronx at the time of my arrest had the Bronx House, which is currently closed down but now the Bronx has the Riker's Island Barge (aka) V.C.B.C.C, Vernon C Bain Correctional Center / The Boat. Brooklyn has the Brooklyn House, Manhattan has the Tombs, and Queens has Riker's Island & the Queens House, which is currently closed at this time. Riker's Island, house's inmates, from all 5 boroughs! Riker's is like a city within a city. It has 10 different facilities that houses over 15,000 inmates. Among the Riker's facilities are a jail for sentenced males, another for sentenced and detainee females, and a detention center for adolescent males (ages 16 to 18). The seven other jails on the Island house adult male detainees. You have Anna M. Kross Center (AMKC), Eric M. Taylor Center (EMTC) Formerly known as CIFM, George Motchan Detention Center (GMDC), George R. Vierno Center (GRVC), North Infirmary Command (NIC), Otis Bantum Correctional Center (OBCC), Robert N. Davoren Complex (RNDC), West Facility (WF), Rose M.Singer Center (RMSC) which houses female inmates & James A. Thomas Center (JATC) which is currently closed. At the time of my arrest I have never been on Riker's Island and truth be told I didn't want to go either. That place was like gladiator school. The stories, that was told about what goes on in there was unimaginable. People getting they face cut over the use of the phones, some for they sneakers, gold chains, and even for commissary you name it, it was happening in every building. It didn't matter how big or small or tough you thought you was somebody was going to try you. Riker's Island was a place that turned some boys to men, men to girls and some girls to men. Unfortunately for me I was sent to MDC and was due back in court September 1st, which was only in 2 days. Really at the time I didn't care where I was sent to I just wanted to get to a bed and get some sleep after laying on them hard ass cells floors for 2 days. The very next morning my bail was posted and I was back on the streets anyway.

CHAPTER 3

I was born to a Harriet Denise Hough, in 1975 on December 25th at 12:52 pm Christmas Day inside of Harlem Hospital, but I was raise in the heart of New York City, a borough called the Bronx's better known as the BX. I grew up in a pretty tough neighborhood. Where respect wasn't giving to you, you had to earn it. I was the oldest out of 4 siblings. My mother was a single parent, trying to raise 3 boys and 1 girl. With no job, it was kind of hard for her taking care of 4 kids on her own. When I was 2 years old my father moved with his parents to Baltimore Maryland to escape the Heroin drug trade that was going on in Harlem in the late 70's. My grandmother, on my father side was deep in the game so was my father and his brothers. She hustled in the streets of Harlem amongst the notorious African-American New York-based criminal organization known as The Council. The Council was a drug and crime syndicate in New York City created by Harlem gangster Nicky Barnes in the 1970s. Growing up without that father figure in my life was kind of difficult for me! Whatever my mother couldn't teach me I learned from the streets. When I turned 7 years old my mother took, my brothers, my sister and me to live down south. We stayed with one of my aunts for a few months until she was able to get a place of her own. We moved into one of them Trailer Park Houses in a small town called Lamar, in South Carolina. We lived there for about 2 years before returning back to NYC due to my youngest brother asthma. We stayed with my grandmother until my mother found her own apartment further uptown in the Bronx's on Kingsbridge Rd. I decided to live with my grandmother when my moms moved into her new place. I grew up like every normal kid I loved to play sports especially football & baseball. I figure the NFL or MLB was the only way I could make it out the hood successfully. When I was younger I did play for little league's Football & Baseball teams. My favorite 2 athlete's were Lawrence Julius Taylor from the New York Giants and Don Mattingly from the New York Yankees. The junior High school I attended didn't have either activity so after I graduated I tried to go to a High school that did. The 3 High schools I applied for was DeWitt Clinton, John F.

Kennedy & Grace Dodge. The only High School I was accepted by was Grace Dodge but they didn't have Football Only baseball, which was only varsity. After being in Dodge for 2 semesters I kind of loss interest in playing any sports. During the summer vacation it wasn't much for us to do but just hang around in the neighborhood. The building I lived in with my grandmother was a well, known weed spot. All day long customers flowed in and out the building so much you would of thought they lived there. As I hung out I started to recognize their face's more & more where as I started directing traffic. I would let them know if it was too hot for them to go up in the building or even let them know that Dred step out for a few. Dred was a shotta, an original gangsta from Craig Town Jamaica. Jamaica is one of the most violent countries in the world, on a level with South Africa and Colombia. Dred migrated to the states back in 1990 to escape the violence and poverty that went on in his country. New York City was his new home and all he seen was bright lights & big dreams. It got to the point whenever Dred left I would tell him to leave me a few bags to do while he was gone since I knew most of the customers. At first I just did it to hold Dred down so the flow wouldn't die out, but every time he left a package it would be done by the time he came back. That's when he started giving me a percentage off each pack I was hook after that. Dred had customers coming from all over the city even from New Jersey, and those were the big spenders. Them white boys was coming to get 40 & 50 bags at a time at least 3 and 4 time a week. I wasn't the only one hustling out there at the time so when them white boys pulled up niggas was fighting for that sell. Back then Police didn't really care to much about locking people up for weed, unless you got caught with a large amount. Whenever blue & white did jumped out to search us, if we had more then 5 bags on us they just made us toss whatever we had inside the sewer, shit I didn't mind, as long as we wasn't going to jail. At first that weed money was helping out a lot but then I started to need more money. I started hugging the block more skipping school just to hustle. I was the type if I didn't have nothing new to wear to school I didn't go. My grandmother never knew if I went to school or not she left the house every morning for work at 5:15am and didn't get home until 4:30pm. She worked at one of those Marriott Hotels in mid-town Manhattan as a head cook. As I hugged the block more i started seeing more money and the fresher I got. My Grandmother started to notice me coming in the house with newer sneakers and cloths and always asked where did I get them sneakers. I always told her I found money inside the hallway or I won money playing dice, she always went for it up until one day I fucked up and left my weed stash inside the mailbox. I was so high one day I forgot to move it before she came home from work. She called me right upstairs and asked me who stuff was that in her mailbox, which I stated I was holding it for a friend. After that I never let her catch me slipping again. A few months later shit really got real when Dred got murdered. My niggas & I was cutting school hanging out in front of my building that morning shooting dice. Dred was sitting on a crate about 10 feet away from us sipping on A Guinness Stout when some nigga hopped out of a car, yelling stop the bank. As we all looked, all I seen was somebody with a mask on they face clutching a big ass chrome long nose 357 in their hand. My first thought was he was coming to stick up the dice game and rob us for our weed, but he ran right pass us toward Dred who was sitting on the crate. Dred was sitting there talking to a customer, he never seen him coming because if he did that situation might have been much different. Dred was a gangsta for real but that day he died with his gun in his waist. They say if you live by the gun, you'll die by the gun and that's the way he went out. Not one bag of weed was sold the rest of that day in honor of my nigga Dred. A lot of people came through that day to pay their respect Dred was a good nigga in the hood. Slowly but surely that flow Dred build died when he past away. Dred had a lot of personal customers that only brought weed from him so once they heard of his passing they stop coming around as well. Dred was the Connect, so when he got killed, it was time to switch hustle's.

CHAPTER 4

I took my hustle up the block, where the older heads from my hood hustled. The corner up the block had that different type of bread coming through there, they had that crack & dope money flow. I didn't know shit about selling dope and to tell you the truth i didn't want to know either. In my hood we had a mutual agreement with each other, the Puerto Ricans had the dope and the black's had the crack to avoid any conflict. When I came on the scene niggas was still selling bottles. It was like 4 different colors on the block. Niggas used different colors to distinguish the different type of work they had. My nigga mizzal had orange tops. While everybody on the block sold treys my nigga mizzal was selling 2 for three's, which is 2 bottles for $3.00. He was killing the competition, 2 for 3 and the work was butter. Fiends was going crazy they couldn't believe it. Mizzal was my nigga so it was only right i team up with him, plus he had a mean flow. We had the illest gimmick's out, but some fiends always tried to get over on us. They could never come with straight paper. Some came with $2.50, $2.75, even $2.00 so what we did is if you didn't have the whole $3.00 you got one bottle. Now we had Duce's too, so if you wanted that 2 for 3 deal you better had straight paper. Back then when David Dinkins was Mayor that cocaine was coming through like crazy and it was cheap, but as soon as Rudy Giuliani got in office things started to change up a bit coke prices started to raise. In 1993, Dinkins lost to Republican Rudy Giuliani in a rematch of the 1989 election. Under Dinkins' Safe Streets, and Safe Cities program, crime in New York City decreased more dramatically and more rapidly, both in terms of actual numbers and percentage, than at any time in modern New York City history. The rates of most crimes, including all categories of violent crime, made consecutive declines during the last 36 months of his four-year term, ending a 30-year upward spiral and initiating a trend of falling rates that continued beyond his term. In 1994, William Bratton, was appointed the 38th Commissioner of the NYPD by Mayor Rudolph W. Giuliani. He cooperated with Giuliani in putting the broken window theory into practice. The broken window theory is a criminological theory of the Norm-setting and signaling effect of urban disorder and vandalism on additional crime and anti-social behavior. The theory states that maintaining and monitoring urban environments in a well-ordered condition may stop further vandalism and escalation into more serious crime. Shit started to get real crazy in the City. Coke got so expensive at one point we had to stop using bottles and start bagging up our drugs in little baggie's, which we call slabs. We went from selling Duce's & Treys to Nickels & Dimes now. Using slabs made it easier for us to bag up instead of using bottles, and for us to stash. Them bottles was kind of harder to hide, you couldn't keep that many on you at a time, as for them slabs we was holding at least 30 to 40 bags on us at one time. I had the perfect stash right there in my ass crack (no freaky) police wasn't hip to that we called that cheeking up. Tuesday's & Thursday's in my hood was the 2 days out the week you had to be real careful out their hustling. They had a tactical narcotic's team better known as (TNT) that flood the streets with undercover officers who conduct so-called buy & bust operations, arresting mostly low -level drug dealers. In my hood we have 1 main rule we go by to avoid all that buy & bust going to jail shit, (**don't serve anybody you don't know**). Most of the time we just shut it down if it got too hot. They started to get slick on us and started sending crack heads with the mark bills. As time progressed I was getting older, old enough where as I develop a responsibility I had to take on where I needed more money & hustling for niggas wasn't cutting it I needed my own work. I had a girlfriend who was pregnant at the time and her mother had kicked her out her house due to her pregnancy and now was living with me. We were both too young to be thinking about having a kid but this was her second time pregnant and we weren't about to abort this one. At that time she was only 16 and I was 18 but we thought we was both grown. I had moved out of my grandmother house & started living with my aunt who had a 3 Bedroom apartment on the same block with my grandmother. The older heads in my hood had a little animosity toward me and my nigga's about getting our own work & hustling on the block. They acted like they wanted us to hustle for them forever. One thing for sure Two things for certain we wasn't having that at least I wasn't. When I first got in this game I use to dream about being a boss I couldn't wait to be able to own a block and just give out packs to all my workers. The older heads were whom I wanted to be like. They had about no less then 20 workers working for them, I know, I was one of them. As I look back at it now they wasn't wrong at all on how they felt. We got into it with them a few times but nothing, that serious where as gunplay had to get involved but if it had to come to that point believe me we was up & ready. One of my mans from the hood name Dollars (R.I.P) who is now passed away, had a brother that moved out of town to Connecticut sent word back that it was money out there and that the town was wide open. Dollars put me & my nigga D.P on about it and ask us did we wanted to go out there and check it out, we jump right on it. First thing we did was we went straight to Broadway and brought some coke. After walking up & down Broadway for like a 2 hours we finally found A connect with a good price. He gave it to us at $20 dollars a gram, we was hype. We thought we were getting over on him but in reality he got over on us. We got back to my crib and bag all that shit up. Our nickel bags were going for $20 out there I couldn't believe it. We bagged up about 200 nickel's brought us a couple bags of smoke and was on our way.

CHAPTER 5

New Britain is a city in Hartford County it's located approximately 9 miles southwest of Hartford, with a population of the city about 73,206. New Britain has the largest Polish population of any city in Connecticut. The racial make up of the city is 61% (white), 47%, (non Hispanic) which out of that 47% only 10% is (African American). It took us about 3 hours on the Greyhound to get to the town, we arrived a little after 12am that morning. We hop off that bus 6 deep in a unknown town, and the only thing we knew was, we heard it was some money out here and it was up to us either to get it or not. Not one of us was grippy (packing a gun) that night all we had on us was box cutters & knives. We didn't know a soul in that town we barely knew what direction to start walking in once we got off the bus. The bus station was located in Downtown New Britain, on west main street in front of a Smoke shop call JIMMY'S and right across from the bus station was a 24 hour diner called Miss Washington Diner we went into. I don't even think any of us were hungry but we all agreed so that's where we went. It must be true what they say about New Yorkers, that you can spot a New York nigga from a mile away. As we sitting at the table waiting for our food in comes a black female name Sindi Mitch. Now Sindi knew dam near everybody in that town, so she knew off top we wasn't from there. She spotted us sitting at the table on her way to the restroom. On her way out she made it her business, to make a stop at table and ask was we from New York. I was the first to reply like, yea why what' up! She said she knew it just on how we was dress and the way we talked plus she never seen us before. My man, D.P ask her how far was North & Spring Street from the diner. North & Spring street was the strip we was looking for, we wasn't even far the strip was about a 5 minute walk if that long. Sindi walked with us personally and showed us where it was. She also hooked us up with a safe haven for the night. A Safe Haven is basically a crib if we needed to use if the strip got too hot for us. The strip was wide open it was niggas out there from all parts of the town even niggas from Hartford was out there. We posted up right there on the corner by some bar by the name of FOXY LADIES on Union & Spring Street. My first sell was for $50, by some polish Pollock in an old ass ford escort that wanted 3 for $50 I was hype after that. Dollars brother wasn't lying it was money out there, the town was booming. We finish all 200 bags by 5:00am that morning, even after finding out the work we had was pure garbage, we got what we paid for (SMH). We made a mental note of that and refuse to ever cop work from Broadway again. It was a 6:35 am Greyhound headed for New York City that morning so we waited inside JIMMY'S Smoke Shop until that bus arrived. Once we hit the city my nigga D.P & me made plans to go right back out there that night. Around 3pm that afternoon we called up an O.J to take us to 145th & Amsterdam we had to get some work. A O.J was one of them gypsy cab service's nigga's in the hood like to use, for, #1 they let you smoke in the whip and, #2 you can put them on hold for a hour or more for one set price. A gypsy cab is an illegal unlicensed taxicab and while most jurisdictions require taxicab operators to be licensed, many unlicensed cabs are personal vehicles used by individual to offer unauthorized taxi like services. The nigga driving the OJ put us on to a spot on 141th & Amsterdam to a Dominican name Premo. Premo had that butter cook up. Before we headed back out to Connecticut that night we gave one of our hood fiends a sample and let them test it out. Our last time out in Connecticut we put our work in pink bags but not this time we switched up to green that Broadway bullshit gave pink a bad name. A lot of niggas in the town didn't use baggie's they just broke it off the gram as costumers came. Them niggas was smart though doing it that way it avoided them from catching a possession w/ intent to sell charge to only being charge with having a possession. Not for nothing that's what separated us from them, that work we brought from Premo gave us a name them rock stars was asking for us personally. Every night we stepped off that bus we was risking our lives and our freedom. We ran the same routine for about a month straight coming out there at night leaving in the morning up until we got ourselves a trap house. During our little 30 days run back and forth to Connecticut we got into some drama this one particular night. It was a night we came back to Connecticut after being in the city for 2 days because we couldn't get any work. One of those nights while we was up in the city some niggas from Hartford, came through and robbed everybody on the strip. They had niggas face down on ground in all that, I even heard one nigga got pistol whip that night. So the night we got out there it was wild extra niggas out there I never seen before. It was this one Spanish kid tho, he was feeling some type of way about the situation now that i think about it he might of been the one that got pistol whip out. We never saw this kid before out here so he didn't know us at all. As we walking through the strip this Mother fucker backs out a 12 Gauge saw off shotgun on us talking crazy. He had the drop on us lucky he was on his talk shit first squeeze later. He thought we were one of them Hartford niggas that came through there the other night. I told homie straight up we from New York we out here to get money we not on no robbing shit, this one kid step up and vouch for us saying he been seeing us out there every night for a few weeks. God was with us that night but after that incident it was time to never leave home without it, I refuse to get caught slipping again.

CHAPTER 6

Our first trap house was on 69 Oak St a block off of North Street in New Britain Ct. We met a lady name Thelma who welcome us in and let us trap out of her house. Thelma had 3 kids 2 boys and a teenage daughter. Her daughter who was about 16 years old was the only one living with her the boys lived with their father. Thelma crib wasn't a spot at all she just let her peoples come through every now and then to get high as long as they had something for her. It wasn't No real money coming through there so we still had to play the strip from time to time. We started directing traffic from the strip straight to the house. One thing about buying drugs from off the strip you always have to worry about getting beat for your money. Some niggas be out there selling whatever look like crack they didn't care. Them rock stars will get all the way home and find out they got beat and be piss the fuck off. So once they started to find out they can come to Oak street and buy from us plus get high in the house they felt more comfortable. Within a months time we had Oak Street jumping. We slowed up all that strip money we even had fiends running all the money to the spot just for a hit. Oak street became a gold mine for us, we had so much money running through there Thelma daughter, Special K wanted a piece of the action. She started skipping school just to hustle. Special K had a girlfriend name Melly who mother was very verbally abusive when she drinks, so Melly left home and started staying with Special K. We started taking K & Melly down with us to the city so they can bring the drugs back for us on the bus when it was time for us to re-up.

CHAPTER 7

The weather started to change up & winter was here in full effect. It was time for me to fall back from Connecticut for a little while my girlfriend was due to give birth soon. My son was born January 16, 1995 at 8:32pm I was a proud parent that night. It was a Monday evening and it had been raining off & on all day long so I was up in the crib a little early. We both were laid up in the bed watching a movie when her water broke. I can't even front she was way more calmer then I was, you should of seen how fast I got dress. The only thing on my mind was getting her to the hospital. I was about to call us a cab but my aunt suggested we walk so I just called her mother to let her know we was on our way to the hospital. Bronx Lebanon is one out of 11 Hospitals in the Bronx she chose to give birth in. One thing I regret is not watching her give birth to my son. I was by her side the whole entire time she was going through her contractions but when that time came for her to start pushing I couldn't stomach the sight of that shit. Back then only one parent was allowed in the delivery room so I spin up outta there and let her moms be inside the room with her. I was still a proud father my son was healthy and had all 10 fingers and 10 toes. My son was a Jr. now I had someone to live for, it was time to do right and get out these streets and get a job. After about 1 month or so of filling out applications, back & forth on different interviews, I landed a job working at Au Bon Pain as a sandwich maker on West 4th and Broadway. Au Bon Pain is a French bakery that sells fresh baked bread Cookies, Muffins, Scones, Croissants and specialty bake goods as well as cafe. The pay suck my check's was looking like shit I just knew it wasn't going to last long. I finally quit after working for about 2 months. I was a sick of making sandwiches all fucking day. These wasn't no ordinary sandwiches either you buy from your local bodega or supermarket. I was making sandwiches like Thai Peanut Chicken Wrap, shit be made with (all natural chicken, field greens, tomatoes, cucumbers, carrots, crispy wontons & Thai peanut dressing. I had to remember all that shit too. I had to know which sandwiches get field greens lettuce, which one get Romine lettuce shit like that man o man I was fucking them white people sandwiches up. That 4pm - 12am shift was killing me taking up too much of my time, I was getting home round 1:30am - 2:00am every night and as soon as I fall asleep my son was waking up for a bottle. I wanted nothing but the best for my son but them Au Bon Pain checks wasn't about franks I had to go.

CHAPTER 8

Spring of 1995, my son was starting to get big he was already going on 4 months and I was right back in the streets again. He was still waking up all hours of the night for his bottle so I didn't want to go back out of town just yet. I was back in the hood with it. In my hood it was 3 older heads that really had the block on smash that was their corner, which they inherited. They put their time in out there, blood, sweat, and tears. I was just a young nigga on the come up I wasn't looking at it like that I just wanted to get money. We came to an agreement that we can all get money together. At the time I thought it was a good idea but shit went sour after a few months. Niggas started playing around with that cash so I took my cut and bounce. Me & my niggas decided to start doing our own thing down the block in my grandmother building niggas couldn't tell me nothing down there. We separated ourselves by putting our work in yellow bags since up the block had green & orange. We was the main hustlers on the block so we knew all the customers anyway, so by the time the summer came in we had a nice little flow coming down the block. One night I was out on the block chilling with my nigga Pretty P & Mista-D we shooting the shit blowing it down when this nigga Pretty P like he knew a spot upstate where nigga's could get some more money. All I heard was more money and new town my antennas went straight up. " So I ask where at? " the nigga says Goshen New York his Pops live out there. Now when we were a little younger way before all this hustling shit the nigga Pretty P did move upstate with his pops for a couple of years to go school up there. Now in my head I'm like "dam Goshen NY" I ask him how far is that shit? "The nigga say 1 hour and a half." Mista-D ask do he know how to get there he replied 87 North. That following night we were on our way out there just the 3 of us. Back then Mista-D was the only nigga in our crew with a whip and a license. My nigga had the Audi 5000. I remember that car, nigga's use to always crack jokes about it all the time. It was a bum ass Tuesday night the block was dry, no money coming through. I don't remember who said what, but all I knew was Mista-D was with it and we jump right on the highway. We was 3 deep riding dirty and it was like 11:30pm when we left, we wasn't even on the road 30 minutes and got pulled over that should have told us something but we didn't listen. We weren't too far from Spring Valley I remember just seeing the exit sign. We had just finish smoking on a blunt so the car wasn't all the way aired out yet. As the State Trooper approach the window first thing he ask for was license & registration. As Mista-D passing the paperwork he ask what was the reason we was being pulled over, the officer replied that we was speeding. He walked back to his cruiser to write us up a ticket so we can be on our way. We sat there for about 10 - 15 minutes when another state trooper pulled up in front of us, both officers got out and approach the car. We were asked to step out the vehicle one at a time so they can search us. The first officer said he had smelled marijuana so that gave them probable cause to search the car. I wasn't worry at all about them finding anything in the car we had all our drugs on us cheeked up. They did a quick sweep of the vehicle and let us go. This nigga Mista-D though was acting a little too extra relieved when they didn't find anything in the car. Come to find out it was something in that car they just over looked it, this nigga had his burner stash in the backseat somewhere. Only thing I was a little mad about is that he didn't tell us it was back there before we left the city, but we was good though they didn't find it so we kept going. We were about 15 miles away from the town of Goshen when we get pulled over again. We wasn't speeding this time shit was way to dark out there on that highway for that plus, we was on route 17, shit is known for deer's crossing back and forth. Before the trooper even got to the car Mista-D rolled down his window. I'm like dam here we go again but this time it was the trooper that asked us do we know why we was being pulled over. We were told that we were driving with a black eye (meaning the car had a missing headlight). He started asking us a whole bunch of questions like where was we headed, is it any drugs in the car and the last of them all do we have I.D. I had my Taft H.S identification on me so I was good but my nigga Pretty P was the only one without his. The officer told us he was going to run our name just to make sure they check out, give us a quick search then let us go. We agreed fuck it he's not going to find anything at least that's what we thought the last trooper didn't. All of our names checked out none of us had any warrants. He started taking us out the car one at a time searching us. He had us sit on the front bumper of his cruiser while he went through the car front to back, "JACKPOT" in a split second we went from sitting on the bumper of the car to being face down on the side of the highway all could do was shake my head. We laid face down until his back up arrived and transported us to the state troopers barracks on 369 Nininger Road located in Monroe N.Y. We all were charged with Criminal Possession of a Weapon in the 3rd degree (PL: 265.02) class D felony and Unlawful Possession of Marijuana (PL: 221.05). We were stripped searched fingerprinted and had our picture taken and around 3am that morning we was allowed to make 1 phone call. I called my baby mother and let her know that I was arrested Upstate somewhere so she won't be wondering why I didn't bring my ass home that night. 7am that very next morning we were transported over to the Court House in the Town of Monroe. We was arraigned on weapon & marijuana charges and slap with a $2500.00 dollar bail and remanded to the county jail until our next court date, which was on the 27th of July.

CHAPTER 9

The Orange County Jail is located on 110 Wells Farm Rd in Goshen N.Y. It also has a contract with Immigration and Customs Enforcement to hold Detainee's while they are in removal proceeding or awaiting removal from the United States. At the time of our arrest Pretty P was a juvenile so he was sent to the dorms on the side with the adolescent, Mista-D & I was sent with the adults. On the 27th when it was time for us to report back to court my Lawyer told us the only way we can be release if one of us take the weight. Mista-D stepped up and wrote a statement claiming that the gun was his and that Pretty P & I didn't know that the gun was in the car. After sitting in Orange County for 2 week Pretty P & I was release on our own recognizance and was due back in court the 21th of September.

CHAPTER 10

After 2 weeks of sitting in the county jail I was back on the streets. The first of the month was right around the corner, so I needed to get some work fast. I brought me a little 10 grams and made my way back out to Connecticut, Oak street was still rocking. All it took was one flip and I was right back on my feet again. Mista-D came home after doing an extra 2 weeks in Orange County, which he copped out to 5 years probation for that gun charge so I brought him out to Connecticut with me. The summer of 95 was a turning point for me I couldn't win for shit after being home for 30 days I was right back in the system again, this time I was arrested for transporting drugs through the Port Authority. I was giving a $1500.00 dollar bail due to my open case I had out in Orange County, which I posted the very next day. That Friday morning I was due back in court so I woke up a little earlier to give myself some extra time to have a little breakfast, I wasn't sure how long I was going to be in court. I rolled up a nice blunt, some of that African black I brought the night before while I was in Harlem. The weather report said sunny in the high 70's so I figure I'll dress to impress. I threw on a pair of my dark blue denim Guess jeans, a red Nautica Rugby, with my all white with the red check uptown Nikes and my ST. Louis Cardinals Fitted hat. By 8:30am I was already out the door on my way to catch the 4 Train downtown to Manhattan. I arrived at 100 Centre Street a little after 9am, the line was ridiculous but it was moving kind of quick. I couldn't remember what floor I had to go to so I looked on the calendar sheet to see which part my case was being held in. When I stepped inside the courtroom my Attorney was already there, to me that's a sign of a good lawyer. I got her attention from the back of the courtroom to let her know I was there and within 5 minutes we stepped out into the hallway so she can discuss the case over with me. She let me know that I was being indicted and my case was being moved upstairs to Supreme Court. At the time I didn't know what that meant so she told me it was just the Prosecution had enough evidence to try and convict me if I went to Trial. Going to trial was the last thing on my mind I was young, but I wasn't dumb I got caught red handed. I also asked her how much time I was looking at and what was the least I can get out of this situation if i had to plea guilty. Since this was my first drug felony she mention maybe a 1 to 3 years upstate or even 5 years Probation, which I received a few months later down the line.

CHAPTER 11

The summer came and went and it started to get cold again plus the trap house we had out in C.T on Oak street got raided after dam near a year. Melly, Special K, Thelma, and my cousin Smiggs, was the only ones in the house the night it got hit. They found over 50 grams of crack cocaine, $3000.00 dollars in cash and a bunch of drug paraphernalia that night. Everybody was being held on a $100,000 thousand dollar bond. Melly was still an adolescent so she was taken to a juvenile detention center in Hartford Connecticut while Special K and her mother was sent to a women's correctional facility called Niantic. They sent Smiggs to HCC Hartford Correctional Center in Hartford aka the Meadows. It was around the first of the month in December, me & my niggas was out on the block chilling when this grimy old head from the hood name Debo approach me asking do I know how to cook he had a few grams he wanted me to whip up for him. He told me that Pretty P was upstairs already but he didn't know what he was doing. We had this crack head crib up in my grandmother building on the 3rd floor name Red who's apartment they was in, so I goes up there too see what was going on. Once we get up in the apartment this nigga Debo backs out the ratchet on me in the kitchen. He had another grimy nigga with him at the time name Wop. Now Wop always were a grimy nigga that stayed in prison and them 2 niggas together meant nothing but trouble. This nigga Debo had the ratchet pointed at me telling me to get on the floor while Wop tie me up with duct tape. Now Debo was kind of bugged out but he wasn't that fucking crazy I knew he wasn't going to shoot me the nigga lived right next door to me we was neighbors, but I wasn't to sure about Wop he lived down the block whenever he wasn't in prison. Now my whole purpose of going upstairs with Debo is because he said Pretty P was up there fucking they shit up but when I got up there Pretty P wasn't there I mean at that moment I thought he wasn't. As I'm standing in the kitchen Wop walks up behind and yoke me to the ground while Debo held me at gunpoint then duct tape my hands together. Debo then walk me out the kitchen towards the back room. On our way to the back I notice Pretty's P jacket in the living room on the couch along with his boots but still I didn't see no Pretty P. As we get to the bedroom I see Pretty P and crack head Red both on the floor duct taped up. Debo put me on the floor next to Pretty P and duct tape both of my legs so I couldn't get up. Pretty P started wilding out screaming and shit so Debo put duct tape on his mouth to shut him up. After about 15 minutes or so the bedroom door flew open and one of my other niggas J-dog came running in and went straight to the window and jumped out onto the fire escape. Debo came in running after him but by the time he came in the room J-dog was gone. They had just made their first mistake that cost their well plan robbery scheme to go down the drain. They fucked up when they brought J-Dog and D.P upstairs at the same time. They main focus was D.P at the time so they didn't need to bring J-Dog upstairs with him he had just been release from prison after beating trial which he laid up on Riker's Island for 18 months for sells of a firearm and he wasn't even hustling he only been home 5 days prior to that so that gave him enough time to make a move. After J-Dog jumped out the window Wop went downstairs to see if he can catch him. Debo stayed in the kitchen with D.P so that gave Pretty P and me the perfect opportunity to make a move. Pretty P managed to free his hands from the duct tape and bail straight to the window and jumped out leaving me behind. I was only able to free my legs but my arm's was still taped up. As I got up I made my way to the kitchen I see that Debo had D.P at gunpoint face down on the kitchen floor. I had mention to Debo that the police was on the way and I think that it will be in his best interest for him to leave while he still had time he went for it and blew it out the front door. That night Debo & Wop only came off with about $1300.00 dollars between me, Pretty P, and D.P which wasn't even enough to pay for one of their funeral arrangements if they got caught slipping. After that night the guns came out, it wasn't no use for them being up inside the house.

CHAPTER 12

It's been 2 weeks since that incident with Wop & Debo and it's been no sight of either one of them. I was out on the block one early Saturday morning in front of the bodega eating a butter roll drinking on a hot tea with lemon I wasn't strapped but i had my bullet proof vest on. The block was slow as usual just a few customers coming thru here and there, when 4 African men walk pass me & enter the store. As they came out 1 out of the 4 men ask can he use the pay phone that I was leaning on. As he picks up the receiver to the phone he goes in his pocket to retrieve his phone card he pulls out a large wad of cash in the process of doing that. I don't know how much it was but all I seen was, hundred dollar bills. At first I thought nothing of it until he hung the phone up and walked over to the next pay phone about 10 feet away. As he made his way over I told him, "That phone doesn't work" it didn't have a dial tone. It was 5 to 6 pay phones on that corner and not one of the shits worked properly. As I sat there and watch them check each phone individually my mind started rambling with criminal thoughts. Now that 1 phone that I do know for a fact that was working was down on the next corner in front of the weed building, which gave me enough time to make a move, "them niggas about to get booked". I ran around the corner & called my nigga J-Dog out the window & told him to bring that thing down stairs I had a jookz for us. It took about 5 minutes for J-Dog to come down I let him know what it was and he was with it 100%. As we put our scheme together a few niggas from the hood started to come outside, but we was on a solo mission we didn't need no extra help on this one. J-Dog came downstairs with this 22 10 shot rifle we had that niggas brought back from C.T. Since it was 4 of them J-dog suggested we should get another hammer just in case. We went to my Lil man Jamaica crib and grab the 12 Gauge that he had. Lil Jamaica lived right on the corner in one of those private 2 family houses we use to chill on his porch every now and then blowing it down. On his porch was an old ass refrigerator where we us to stash most of our hammers while we out on the block. The 12 Gauge we had was some old ass Browining, BPS pump shotgun it was sawed off but it put in work. We get to Jamaica crib I tell him " go get that I got a jookz " he tells me the only hammer he have at the time was the shottie. I'm not even going lie I didn't even want to use a second hammer but this nigga J-Dog kept pressing the issue about the other hammer I was going to bluff them with a Tropicana Orange Juice bottle through the coat pocket. I knew who had the money so I just needed a nigga to back them down while I hit they pockets. Now I definitely didn't want to use the shottie but that's all he had at the time. The shotgun was kind of fucked up but it still shoot that's all we needed one shot, one kill. In order for it to shoot we had to cock it back first then load the shell into the chamber, because if we load the shell first then cock it back the shell would jump back out. I said fuck it and told Lil Jamaica to go get it since it was 4 of them. This nigga Lil Jamaica fucking cocks back the shottie then put a shell up in the chamber. First thing I ask him was " did you cock it before putting the shell in, " he tells me no! Without checking it myself I takes his word. I tuck's the shottie down my pants and started heading down the steps of his porch. I had on my Columbia rain suits and a pair of my burgundy construction work timberland boots with the steel toes on. As soon as I reached the bottom landing of the porch I heard a big bang (BOOM). The nigga J-Dog was in front of me and as soon as he heard it he backed out that 22 rifle like (WTF). I swear to you not I didn't know where that shit came from, or knew I was shot until I try to walk off. I look down at my foot and seen a big ass hole in the left foot of my boot, I took off running gun in hand in all. I got across the street and realize I still had the shotgun in my hand so I turned around and ran back across the street where I tossed it back to Lil Jamaica so he can put it away. I still had my vest on I had to take that off to before I got to the hospital. As I'm stripping down one of the older heads from the hood pulled up (R.I.P) to my nigga, First & Last like (WTF) happen and told me to jump in his whip. He drove J-Dog and me to the hospital. I call him First & Last because he was the only nigga that I knew that used his government name as his street name. We got to the Hospital, First & Last already let it be known he was not going, in nobody hospital so J-Dog help me out the car into the emergency room. We didn't even stop in the waiting room area we blew it right pass security straight towards the back fuck signing in. As soon as we got to back I made a big scene to put all the attention towards me and started yelling (I'm shot I'm shot) and falls to the floor. About 3 to 4 doctors on duty that morning rush to my aid. It was so much blood in my boot when the doctor started to cut my boot open blood just started pouring out. That's when the pain kicked in it felt like my foot was on fire. The police arrived like a half an hour after asking me all kinds of questions. I knew I could go to jail f I told them I shot myself so I fabricated a whole story about me being a victim of an attempted robbery. I even gave them a bogus location where it took place. I stayed in the hospital 3 days before being discharged. Christmas was just a week away and I Be dam if I'm laid up in somebody hospital for my 21th birthday that wasn't happening.

CHAPTER 13

1996

I spent my Christmas & New Years in the house with my family I wasn't able to go out but I was still able to turn up but only on 1 foot. I just knew 1996 was going to be a good year for me it couldn't get any worst then 1995, little did I know 95 was just the beginning of my downfall. After about a month I got tired of sitting around the house doing nothing plus I needed to get back on my feet I wasn't making no money sitting around. My nigga's was back in New Britain turning it up niggas found a new spot on Gladden Street in this lady name Reese crib it was rocking too all I needed was somebody to meet at the Jimmy's Smoke Shop when I got off the bus cast in all I was out there. I wasn't even out there a good 30 days yet when my baby mother told me I had a letter in the mail from the Department of Probation telling me the date I had to report. This was my first visit since I copped out to 5 years probation for that case I caught in the Port Authority. I still had about 2 weeks before that date came so that gave me about 2 or 3 more flips. My Probation officer was a lady name, Ms. Cambell she was a brown skin heavy set female in her 30's she was cool tho. I let her know I smoke weed, she didn't give a fuck about that as long as I wasn't on that other shit. She did tell me that I couldn't leave the state of New York under no circumstances, without permission and I had to report every week. Another blow to the gut I just couldn't win for shit. I was back in the hood again for about 2 months straight plus this P.O bitch still had me reporting every week. The block was popping, but it wasn't that C.T money. One day my nigga Black pulled up with this chick name method from New Britain they came down to re-up. Black was on the run he had escape from juvenile detention center upstate we he was 15 years old. Him and J-Dog had caught a ATF case for selling a 22 hand gun to an informant name July that was working for the Feds but the case never went federal the state took the case. Black was sentence to 18 months but only did about 8 months of that. Black been in C.T every since he been home, he came down to cop like 50 grams and was trying to get me to ride back out with him. He told me crack head Reese had a new crib over on Beaver Street I could start it up if I wanted too. Reese crib wasn't a spot yet but it was most definitely about to be one. I swear to you not it was like everywhere them New York boys went the flow followed. All we had to do was let one street hustling crack head know where we were at and they would run everything to us. It took about a week before Reese crib was turned out. Niggas had a couple of spot through out the town J-Dog was up in Mount Pleasant aka (Killa-Hill) Black had a crib over on south main with his girl Melly and a trap spot on Glen Street. Shit started to get crazy over on Beaver Street so Reese shut it down, lucky right before she did that we found us our own crib over on Orange Street. It was J-Dog, Black, Pretty P and me we all agreed to split the rent or take turns paying the shit was only $600 a month for a 3 bedroom. Rule #1 (Never Sell Crack where you rest at)! We started to get real comfortable going out to clubs partying, me and Pretty P even had our girlfriends from the city come up out there. The landlord didn't really want us in that apartment he was hoping that the person that was originally staying there couldn't come up with the rent money so he can get rid of him. The Landlord made a deal with us he told us we can stay in that apartment for another month and that he will give us another apartment in one of his other building on the same block only it's a 2 bedroom. October came in and we finally had a place of our own, we started to send for more niggas in the hood to come up & get money. We had my nigga Topboss and Shortz come up & Pretty P had one of his side chicks come up there with him for his birthday week. First shit we agreed on was not to have any traffic coming through there at all this is where we laid our head at but this one fiend we called Chi-town came banging on our front door talking about he had $80. I don't know how the fuck he found out where we lived at but he did and from there on out I knew we was fucked. I backed the hammer right out on him "Who da fuck told you we stay here"! I told him to get the fuck out of here & don't ever knock on this door again! The whole time I had the hammer in his face. It was a blue minivan parked out front on the other side of the street by the funeral home I paid it no mind I wanted to see what car Chi-Town got in. Chi-Town went in the whole opposite direction so he wasn't with them at least that's, what I thought.

CHAPTER 14

Right after that incident with Chi-Town niggas needed to relax they mind so niggas had got a cipher popping! That nigga Pretty P had some of that 124th & Madison that Brown Body Bag some Official Chocolate with him. Right after the cipher everybody went there separate ways. J-Dog was trying to go down to the city and re-up he wanted Special K and me to ride with him I wasn't with it Special K went. Black & Melly went home and Topboss went back to Beaver Street. I was high as hell we smoked like 10 Blunts back 2 back. Last thing I remember was laying on the couch talking to Shortz and Pretty P, his lady friend was in the kitchen making hamburgers before I passed out. It felt like I was sleep for 10 minutes when our front door came crashing in. All I heard was "SEARCH WARRANT everybody get down". I was so high I couldn't even move I thought I was dreaming shit wasn't No dream tho. They tore up the crib for like 2 hours before they took us downtown to the station. We got Charged with numerous charges the next morning The Hartford Courant newspaper article Read: A late night raid Wednesday at an Orange Street drug den ended with the Arrest of 4 people from New York City and confiscation of 2 handguns some crack cocaine and marijuana police said: T. Moore 19, Pretty P 18, T. Hough 20, Shortz 26, all from the Bronx were each charged with possession of narcotic's, Possession of marijuana, possession of drug paraphernalia and operating a drug factory, police said Hough and Shortz were also charged with criminal possession of a firearm. Our Bond was set at $100,000 a piece, up until we got arraign in front of a Judge. Shortz bail and mines drop down to $50,000 & Pretty P and his lady friend bond drop to $20,000. Our next court appearance was set in November I was all the way stress now plus my son Christening was on the 30th of October, (SMH) another blow. Pretty P, Shortz and me were sent to Hartford County and Pretty P lady friend was sent to Niantic. As soon as we got process they split us up and sent us each to different dorms. I don't remember where they went but I went to dorm 3 where the whole set up was bunk beds. You had 100 inmates in one dorm, 4 man cubes and 8 man cubes. The C.O's that ran the housing unit assign which cube and bunk you sleep in I was sent to a 4 man, cube I was good. After getting my shit together I went up in the bathroom and on my way out guess who I run into this grimy nigga Wop. Last time I seen this nigga is when him & Debo pull that bullshit on us up in Red crib. I heard he was back out in New Britain, niggas had brought him out there back when Oak Street was jumping he got jammed up fucking around on the eastside. "What's up Gotti" was the first thing he says to me! "Nigga you know what's up you & your man Debo did that bullshit! " The nigga started laughing like shit was a joke, word!!!! The nigga tells me it was all Debo idea that night to run down on niggas & the hammer Debo had didn't even work. Debo even pull a fast one on him that night about how much cash they came off with. We chopped it up for like an hour until the lights went out. I wasn't even in Hartford County 48 hours before being transferred to Corrigan Correctional Institution out in Uncasville Connecticut. Corrigan was straight lock down all cells 23 hours lock down with 1 hour, recreation. During that 1 hour you had to take your shower, use the phone or make you something to eat it was your choice. J-Dog & Black had already bonded Pretty P out his bond was only $20,000 and 10% of that was $2,000. When Pretty P got out the plan was for him to help J-Dog & Black get me out next then Shortz since we had the highest bonds. The night of the raid police never found my grams I had stash outside the window pane I watched them search through the entire house so my money was good, but for some reason they said my work wasn't there when nigga's looked. I'm not pointing the finger at anyone but everybody in that house knew where I stash my work. My son Christening was right around the corner and I'm still sitting in jail. I'm calling home and niggas is telling me they waiting on this person to come up with they half of the money or this person is not around all the riff shit I didn't want to hear. My baby mom's and her family had this Christening planned for some time now and it was to late to try and cancel it, it was going down with or without me. J-Dog was my son godfather so he had to be there to represent, Pretty P, Butter and P.O.P also was there on my behalf. The day of my son christening I just sat in my cell thinking to myself how my life was taking a major turn for the worst. I was already in violation of my probation by leaving the state of New York without permission then on top of that I get arrested for operating a drug factory with 2 firearms I was fucked. I told my baby mother to contact my P.O and let her know that I was locked up since it wasn't looking like I was going to make bond I already miss my initial report date. They woke us up at 3:30am for court and we sat in the bullpens to around 6:30 – 7am before being transported back over to Hartford County so we can catch the bus going to New Britain courts. The judge on the bench that day was on some real bullshit for one he wouldn't lower our bond and he set our next court date all the way in January next year but he did let Pretty P lady friend release with time serve and a promise not to return to the state of Connecticut after her 30 something days stay. My lawyer said the D.A was being a hard ass because we were from New York City. My entire family and friends were in the court room that morning my mother, baby mother, sister, uncle, and aunt but it didn't matter tho the only way I was walking out that court room unless I made bond. After our case was called we was sent back to the bullpens so we can be transported back to the county jail. As we waited a Bondmen from B&B came to the back handing out business cards I ask him what would he take for a $50,000 bond he said $3,500 with 3 signatures. I told him I was from the city he said it didn't matter he was willing to work with me. I told him my peoples were out in front and for him to see what are they working with as far as bond money. I don't know what they had but it wasn't no $3,500. I had made a promise to pay him $100.00 a week up until my next court date. My mother was the first one to sign her John Hancock I don't remember who was the other 2 people that signed their signatures but I really did appreciate it.

CHAPTER 15

Once again I'm home after 30 something days out in Connecticut. First thing I did the next morning was, go see my probation officer. I explain to her the situation about the case and that I was helping a friend move from New Britain back to NYC when the apartment was raided. She could have violated me but she didn't she just told me to stay out of C.T unless I had to go back to court. My favorite 3 holiday's was around the corner, Thanksgiving, Christmas and New Years Eve. Now it's never a good time to be in jail but you definitely don't want to be locked up during these holidays it's the worst feeling ever. I like to be around nothing but family kicking back chilling, smoking, and drinking, not on my bunk, playing chess, cards, or in some fucking dayroom with a bunch of niggas. Plus Christmas was my birthday who the fuck want to be in jail on they born day I know not me that's who, but little did I know I was about to spend a few birthdays on somebody's bunk in a cell. Thanksgiving was a blast, now it was time for me to gear up for my 21th birthday Christmas was a week away and I wanted to do it big I was legal now (LMAO) even though I've been doing what I wanted too but it was official. It was lit for my 21th b-day I don't remember much what I did but all I know is that I had a ball that night because I woke up the next day broke. I had drugs and just enough money to buy me a butter roll and a hot tea with lemon. I got up early that morning and hit the block. Once I got to the block the homie Monster G who is no longer with us (S.I.P) was the only person out there. We was chilling in front of the weed building when this nigga Pretty P pulled up in a half of G (crack head rental) he got from a fiend out in New Britain. Monster G wanted to go get some chocolate they had uptown on Briggs so Pretty P let us hold the whip while he ran upstairs to his crib. We pulled up on Briggs & Monster G hops out and runs in the building. While Monster G was up in the building the D's rode pass me 3 deep in an unmarked vehicle while I was double parked". It took about 5 minutes for Monster G to come out of the building and by that time the D's had already spin around the block and was coming back around when Monster G was getting in the whip. I told

40

Monster G to cheek up the boys was right behind us. They let us drive for like 2 blocks before they pulled us over. I already knew the routine so once I pulled over I rode down all the windows and shut the car off, " License & Registration " they ask for. Now back then it wasn't legal to drive w/out a license but as long as you had I.D and knew how to drive properly you was good. I definitely didn't have a license so I pass the officer my Taft H.S identification. Monster G didn't have no type of identification on him, that was strike 1 against him and on top of that he was giving them attitude. I didn't know whose car the name was under so I just told the officer a friend of mines let me hold it to make a quick run. He told us to sit tight while he ran our names to make sure we didn't have any warrants. Now that I knew I didn't have I just came home, so I wasn't too worried. While officer dick head #1 ran our names officer dick head 2 & 3 stood on standby. Officer dick head #2 was on the passenger side fucking with Monster G asking a bunch of questions like " where we coming from?" and also where we going? " Monster G wasn't feeling him at all I started answering all the questions that were being asks. Monster G drew a lot of attention to his self because of his attitude that's when Officer dick head #2 notice a bunch of dried up blood all on his jeans. Now those questions I couldn't answer for him he was on his own. I knew we had a blast last night but I didn't remember putting hands & feet on anybody that night I don't even know if Monster G remembered what happen last night because he couldn't answer where the blood came from either. They made us get out the car while they pat us down for any weapons and search the vehicle. I didn't have shit on me but a Philly blunt cigar, Monster G had about $1500.00 dollars cash in his pocket mostly in singles so it looked like way more, now they want to know where he get all this money from, shit started to look ugly for us. This nigga Monster G had a bunch of dried up blood on him, a pocket full of cash and to top it off the car we was driving had been reported STOLEN! I don't believe this shit not again my heart just drop. They must have thought we just caught a jookz or something because they got on some real bullshit with us. Monster G started wilding out like "Why y'all taking me for I'm not driving I'm just a passenger " they didn't care about none of that they didn't like his attitude from the start. They took us over to the

52nd Precinct on Webster Ave in the Bronx where we was booked, fingerprinted and had our picture taken before we was ship down to central bookings on 161th street. I was charged with Grand Larceny in the 3rd, Criminal Possession of stolen property in he 3rd, Unauthorized use of a vehicle without owner consent. The Grand Larceny charges was drop down because I had the keys but I was charge with Unauthorized use without owner consent and Criminal possession of stolen property. I was piss the fuck off sitting in them pens down in central bookings I wanted to kill Pretty P ass for giving me that hot ass car. Here it is December 26, and I'm back in the system the day after my 21th birthday plus I had another court date coming up on the 3rd of January out in C.T, I couldn't afford to miss or my bond will be revoke. All I was praying for was an (R.O.R) on this case so I can make my court date in Connecticut. If the Judge remanded me on this case I'm fuck unless I get a low bail and bail out before then. By the grace of god I made night court the following night and was release on my own recognizance (SHEESH). The New Year was approaching and everything was just going downhill for me I was wondering was 1997 going to be a better year or my downfall.

CHAPTER 16

It was around 4am in the morning I was up getting ready for court out in New Britain. I had about 2 ½ hours before I caught that 6:30am express bus headed for Connecticut and I still had to purchase my ticket so I had to get going. My bus arrived in New Britain at 8:30am that morning I had more then enough time to grab me something to eat and smoke a blunt before the courts open. I beep my nigga Black to let him know I was in the town so he can pick me up at the bus station. Black had a trap spot around the corner from the bus station on Walnut Street so he pulled right up. The courts started at 10:00am and it was packed too, they were starting the New Year off with a bang. The district attorney acted surprise when my case was called and I approach the bench from the outside, I don't know what the fuck he thought but I wasn't trying to lay up in there. My case was adjourned to a later date in February I just had to stay out of trouble until then. After court J-Dog, Black and me hung out until it was time for me to catch that Greyhound back to the city. I was right back in my same routine again hustling on the block Topboss & Butter was back in the city as well after the raid on Orange Street. My Lil man 2nd birthday was approaching fast and I definitely didn't want to be sitting in nobody jail cell when that day came so I took a little break from the streets. His born day fell on a Thursday so we had a little get together in our house that following weekend. My mother & my sister came through and they also brought my nephew who was 1 years old at the time. The turn out was nice everybody enjoyed themselves my baby moms was happy so was I. 1997 was a cold winter it seem like it snowed every fucking week in February as soon as one snow storm passed another one came that following week Spring couldn't get here fast enough. My grand larceny case was dismissed but I still had that case in C.T I was fighting Shortz had already copped out to 20 months but they was still as trying to give me a asshole full of time. They had offered me

42 months for operating a drug factory and possession of a firearm, which they found my fingerprints on. Shit was starting to get real I needed to get myself a paid lawyer instead of this public pretender I was using. Why was I being offered more time then everyone else I asked myself? Every lawyer I talk to wanted $5,000 to handle my case but they couldn't guarantee I was going to walk without doing any time. Rumors had been circulating through the town that Judge Scheinblum, was returning back to the bench and I didn't want no parts of that man that judge was crazy and out of his mind I had to get my case resolved quick. Judge Scheinblum was some different type of judge he played no games that nigga use to play the violin when he sentence you. One time I heard he told a drug dealer that was in his courtroom " Did you see that tree this morning outside before you came inside the court house? The dealer answered what tree! He said, well it will be one out there by the time you come home! He also use to ask people how many buttons do your shirt have, whatever answer you gave him that's how many years he was going to give you. I made note of that and reminded myself never to where a button up shirt in his courtroom. He wasn't to fond of New Yorkers coming to his town dealing drugs especially after his daughter died of an overdose. I needed a paid lawyer and I needed one ASAP. That nickel & dime money I was making on the block wasn't going to get it back to New Britain it was but this time my baby mother was on some other shit. She didn't like the fact that I was going back out there hustling I couldn't blame her but I had to do what I had to do. By this time it was already spring & a lot of things change. Black had got caught in a raid on beaver Street and was locked up doing 18 months so I didn't really have any input on what was going on in the town. I didn't have a trap house to go to and I wasn't about to play the strip so my nigga Butter & me rented a room in the Ramada Inn and trapped out of there. The Ramada Inn was literally about 50 feet from the police station we was just asking to go to jail. The room in the Ramada was $80 a night that was chump change to us. It was these 2 chicks out there name Bre & Rosemary that we meet back in 1994 when we use to hustle on North Street doing they thing put me on to this chick name Cee-Cee that had her own crib up on Silver Street only thing I had to do was

act like I liked her and take one for the team & the crib was our. After 2 months of trapping out of the Ramada we finally had a crib. Cee-Cee apartment on Silver Street was a 2 bedroom it was perfect for us. Now the plan was not to hustle out of the crib but after a month or so that plan was changed. Once niggas seen we was situated everybody wanted to come back out there it was me, butter, D.P, Smiggs, Mister-D, P.O.P, and my nigga 2 peace we had Silver Street rocking. Around that time coke was now $40 a gram so niggas was bagging up dam near $4,000 off an ounce. A lot of funny business started occurring so niggas split up and went they separate ways, I wasn't going anywhere I found this spot. Cee-Cee had moved out and went to Boston somewhere to live with her aunt & left us the crib that's when shit really got crazy. My court date was approaching and I needed a lawyer bad I was not trying to do 3 ½ years in Connecticut for nobody so all that funny business niggas was pulling I wasn't with it. I found a lawyer that was willing to work with me with a payment plan, he also mention he might can get me a fine with a promise to stay out of C.T for 5 years. I was with that all day, all I had to do was pay a fine and stay out of Connecticut for 5 years let's get it. I gave the lawyer $500 for retainer fee's and told him I had another $500 on my next court date. The morning I was due too appear in court was very hectic they had just did a sweep of the town and arrested over 49 gang members of the Los Solidos. After a 10 Month investigation a total of 76 members of the Los Solidos were sought on charges ranging from murder and racketeering to drug selling and reckless driving. The Los Solidos was a ruthless Puerto Rican gang formed in 1990 out in Hartford C.T. All cases on the docket that morning was push over to the following month. I had at least an extra month to get my shit together and get this chicken up for this lawyer. It was crunch time for a nigga I couldn't worry about nobody else but myself, niggas started beefing and shooting at each other shit was crazy. The landlord was trying to get rid of us he wanted us out of that apartment shit, I couldn't blame him we didn't pay rent the whole time we were living there especially after Cee-Cee left. The time came I was back in court the lawyer I hired kept his word & got me a fine & a promise to stay out of New Britain, not Connecticut tho. The judge ordered me to pay a $3,000 fine and gave me a month to pay. I was happy but if I didn't have that bread by next month I was going to jail. Now I was in debt dam near $7,000 I owed the lawyer $4,000 and the courts $3,000. I wasn't to worried about the lawyer fee's we had an agreement but the courts that was something different I had to get that chicken up for them and had 30 days to do so. I was out there on my grind 24/7. The landlord got his wish and got us the fuck out of there, he sold the whole building and the new owners wasn't playing they gave us 48 hours to move all of our property off the premises. We had a crazy flow coming through there this couldn't be happening not now. The new owners came and put up a fence around the whole building they made sure we didn't sell another bag in that apartment they even put 3 Pit bull terrier inside the fence they wasn't playing. Niggas just got on some real New York shit and open the block up and started playing the corner like we did back in the city. I had to get that $3,000 up before the 13th of August and the 1st of the month was right around the corner. I could tell you this much, we was all out there together but you really was out there on your own when it came to certain situations like the one I was in. Nobody I mean nobody even offered to help me out with getting up that chicken so I could stay my black ass out of jail, that's when I realize friends & business was 2 different things. It's no friends in this business I was on my own. I needed to get at least 2 more flips in before the 13th but the end of the month was really slow. The 1st of the month fell on a Friday and that Sunday I went back down to the city so I could re-up and actually get some well needed rest I've been breaking night for the past 4 to 5 days sleeping in cars whenever I could. I stayed in the city for 2 days & was right back on the grind. I got to the town around 3pm first thing I did was go check my little PYT (Pretty Young Thing) that lived out in Mount Pleasant name Kay, she wasn't home so I swung by her job to let her know I was back in the town. No she wasn't my girl but I did like her little young ass she was up & coming. Kay already had a boyfriend some nigga name Jay-Jay who was about to go away to college to Play basketball. The funny shit is Jay-Jay had a sister name Fendi, who I been trying to get next too for the pass 2 years but her crazy ass baby father was on her back. Fendi had just came home from jail and wasn't fucking with that nigga no more and made plans to get next to me sometime during the week. The streets was hot police had been riding around all day I was just waiting for the sun to go down. I liked when the police came out early I knew they wouldn't be out tonight crashing any cribs. My nigga Pretty P came through Silver Street to check me and smoke something with a nigga I jumped in the whip and we rode around the town. The town was quiet only people out were drug dealers and fiends. We drove through North Street where we ran into Fendi and her best friend Queen C, Fendi was back on the paper chase she wasn't even home 2 weeks yet and was back on it. I don't know about Pretty P but I was trying to play for a few hours a little 1 on 1, Pretty P and Queen C already had they little connection but Fendi had to get home to her kids and gave me a rain check. Pretty P had some bud he got from Hartford, that shit had me litt I fell asleep in the whip and when I woke up the boys was on us. Pretty P tried to jump out and leave me in the car while I was still sleep. That was the second time Pretty P pull some foul shit but the boys was on him, Nah-Nah PaPa "get back in the car" was all I heard. The Car Pretty P was driving had been reported stolen from a dealership out in Bristol Connecticut, they locked his ass up and let me go I was just the passenger joy riding. J-Dog had a crib with his baby mother on Union Street and him and his brother G was out there smoking and seen everything go down, I made J-Dog drive me back to Silver Street it was back to the grind. When I got back to the block 2 Peace was out there holding it down. 2 Peace had rented this white drop top convertible Le Baron from this fiend we just sat in that shit for the rest of the night trapping. We must of both fell asleep because when we woke up police had us surrounded (awww man) not again, but this time we wasn't driving it's not illegal to sleep in a car is it? Neither one of us was dirty so we was good they just check the car and ran our names and made sure that the car we was in wasn't stolen. They told us to get off the block so I made 2 Peace drive me downtown to get a room in the Ramada so I could take a shower. I stayed up in the room for the rest of the day until it was time for me to come back out. I came back to the block around 4:30pm and I let 2 Peace get the room key so he can go take a shower and change his cloths. Mista-D was the only one out there with me when officer Steck and his crew pulled up on us. Steck knew me from the Orange Street raid and hopped out. The only thing I had in my Possession was a set of car keys that went to a Blue Golf Volkswagen we had parked up. I had my work stashed behind one of those private houses on the block so I wasn't worried. They knew we were from New York City so we weren't out there for nothing. Steck took the set of keys out my pocket and started searching the car within 5 minutes he found some work that was stashed inside one of the seats on the passenger side. Since I had possession of the keys nine tenths of the law the car was mines and I was arrested for possession with the intent to sell. What!! That shit wasn't even my work and they were locking me up for somebody else shit I was pissed. They set my bond at $100,000 until I was arraign in front of a judge where he only lowered it down to $75,000 and was sent over to Hartford County until my next court date which was in September.

Epilogue

I couldn't believe this shit once again I was back in the county jail, how the fuck I was going to get out of this one and to make things worst Judge Scheinblum was due to return back to the bench in September. (FUCK FUCK FUCK) I couldn't sit there and cry about the situation I just had to put the (H) on my chest and handle that shit. Them first 30 days was a little rough for the kid I was making a bunch of enemies I already got it on twice with 2 different gang members a Solido and a 20 love member. I was young and disrespectful I didn't give a fuck I was too far away from home to be acting like some pussy nigga not me. The fine I was offered was still on the table but they wanted some jail time too. The District Attorney was on some take it or leave it last offer shit but I had to find out if my probation officer was going to violate me if I take a plea deal. They offered me 18 months with a $3,000 fine I didn't take it, I was trying to get them to put both cases together and pay one big fine so I can walk but the D.A was on his sucker shit. I was not trying to pay a fine and go to jail plus the money I did have was voucher and use as evidence in my case I was back to square one.

TO BE CONTINUE.......

No More State Greens

Contact: nomorestategreens@gmail.com